DISCARD

MOUNTAIN BIKING

BY HOLLIE ENDRES

BELLWETHER MEDIA • MINNEAPOLIS, MN

Are you ready to take it to the extreme? Torque books thrust you into the action-packed world of sports, vehicles, and adventure. These books may include dirt, smoke, fire, and dangerous stunts.

WARNING: read at your own risk.

This edition first published in 2008 by Bellwether Media.

No part of this publication may be reproduced in whole or in part without written permission of the publisher. For information regarding permission, write to Bellwether Media Inc., Attention: Permissions Department, Post Office Box 1C, Minnetonka, MN 55345-9998.

Library of Congress Cataloging-in-Publication Data
Endres, Hollie J.
  Mountain biking / by Hollie J. Endres.
    p. cm. -- (Torque : action sports)
  Summary: "Photographs of amazing feats accompany engaging information about mountain biking. The combination of high-interest subject matter and light text is intended to engage readers in grades 3 through 7"--Provided by publisher.
  Includes bibliographical references and index.
  ISBN-13: 978-1-60014-126-3 (hardcover : alk. paper)
  ISBN-10: 1-60014-126-9 (hardcover : alk. paper)
  1. All terrain cycling--Juvenile literature. 1. Title.

GV1056.E43 2008
796.63--dc22
                                                    2007010300

Text copyright © 2008 by Bellwether Media.
SCHOLASTIC, CHILDREN'S PRESS, and associated logos are trademarks and/or registered trademarks of Scholastic Inc. Printed in the United States of America.

CONTENTS

REACHING THE TOP	4
WHAT IS MOUNTAIN BIKING?	8
EQUIPMENT	12
IN ACTION	16
GLOSSARY	22
TO LEARN MORE	23
INDEX	24

REACHING THE TOP

A mountain biker pumps hard on his pedals as he climbs a steep hill. Loose dirt flies off of the bike's spinning tires. The rider reaches the top of the hill. He's not stopping there.

It's time to cruise down the hill. The rider tucks his head low over the handlebars. The bike flies down the slope. The rider narrowly dodges rocks, tree branches, and steep drop-offs. It took half an hour to climb the hill. It will take just minutes to ride back down at such a fast speed.

WHAT IS MOUNTAIN BIKING?

Mountain bikers ride over rugged **terrain**. Mountain bikes can handle dirt, mud, and rocky surfaces. Riders can take their mountain bikes just about anywhere.

There are two main styles of mountain biking. Cross-country riding is the most popular. Cross-country bikes are lightweight and built for almost any kind of riding. Almost anyone can enjoy cross-country riding.

Downhill riding is a popular sport among more serious riders. These riders need bikes that are heavy and durable. Downhill bikes must be able to take a lot of hard bumps and wipeouts.

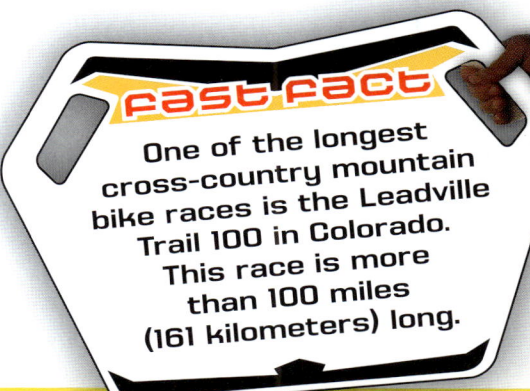

Fast Fact

One of the longest cross-country mountain bike races is the Leadville Trail 100 in Colorado. This race is more than 100 miles (161 kilometers) long.

EQUIPMENT

A mountain bike is a cross between a road bike and a **bicycle motocross (BMX)** bike. It is full-sized with many gears like a road bike. A mountain bike also has a thick frame and "knobby" tires with deep **tread** for gripping rough terrain. Both are characteristics of BMX bikes.

Some mountain bikes have a strong **suspension system** of shock absorbers. Mountain bikes with suspension systems are for extremely rough downhill riding.

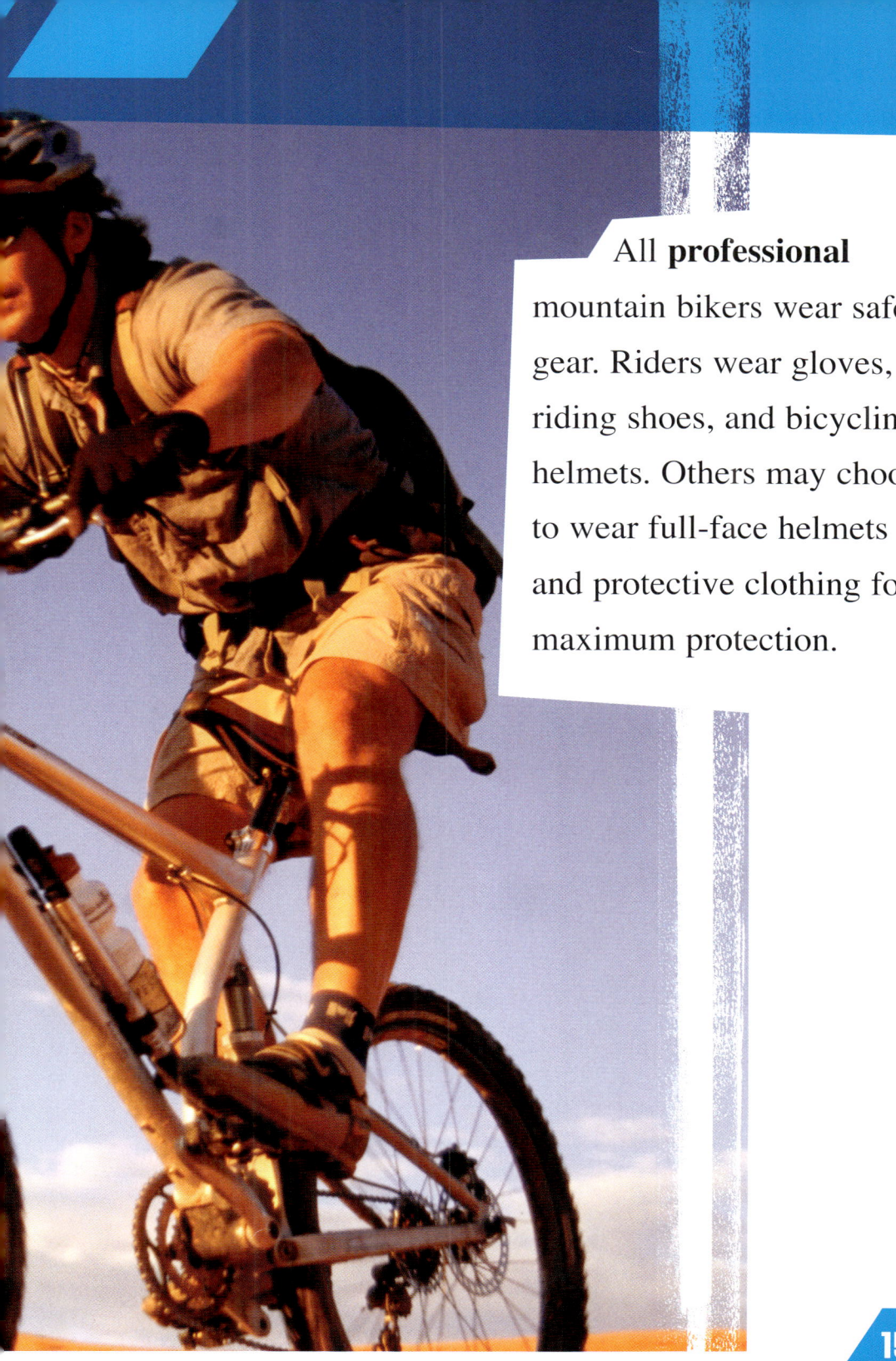

All professional mountain bikers wear safety gear. Riders wear gloves, riding shoes, and bicycling helmets. Others may choose to wear full-face helmets and protective clothing for maximum protection.

IN ACTION

Amateurs and professionals compete in a variety of races. Cross-country races are the most common. Riders race on marked off-road courses. They pedal over rocks, dirt, and mud. They go up and down steep hills. They may even cross small streams.

Downhill racing is also popular. Some downhill events take place on ski slopes after the snow has melted. Other downhill events take place on mountains. Some races require racers to go through gates on their way down the hill.

fast fact

Christian Taillefer set the world record for speed on a mountain bike when he went 131.7 mph (212 km/h) down a glacier!

In other races mountain bikers pedal straight down a steep slope in an all-out sprint! This thrilling and dangerous sport is mountain biking at its most extreme.

GLOSSARY

amateur—a non-professional athlete who competes in a sport

bicycle motocross (BMX)—a sport in which riders race around a dirt track on small, durable bicycles

professional—an athlete who makes money by competing in a sport

suspension system—a series of springs and shock absorbers that connect the body of a mountain bike to its wheels

terrain—the natural surface features of the land

tread—the series of bumps and grooves on a tire that help it grip rough surfaces

TO LEARN MORE

AT THE LIBRARY
Deady, Kathleen W. *Extreme Mountain Biking Moves*. Mankato, Minn.: Capstone, 2003.

Osborne, Ian. *Mountain Biking*. Minneapolis, Minn.: Lerner Publications Co., 2004.

Savage, Jeff. *Mountain Bikes*. Mankato, Minn.: Capstone, 2003.

ON THE WEB
Learning more about mountain biking is as easy as 1, 2, 3.

1. Go to www.factsurfer.com
2. Enter "mountain biking" into search box.
3. Click the "Surf" button and you will see a list of related web sites.

With factsurfer.com, finding more information is just a click away.

INDEX

amateurs, 16
bicycle motocross (BMX) bike, 12
clothing, 15
clunkers, 7
Colorado, 11
cross-country bikes, 11
cross-country racing, 11, 16
cross-country riding, 11
downhill bikes, 11
downhill racing, 19
downhill riding, 11, 14
gears, 12
glacier, 19
handlebars, 6

Leadville Trail 100, 11
professional, 15, 16
protection, 15
road bike, 12
safety, 15
shock absorbers, 14
ski slopes, 19
suspension system, 14
Taillefer, Christian, 19
terrain, 9, 12
tread, 12
wipeouts, 11

The photographs in this book are reproduced through the courtesy of: Kinetic Imagery, front cover; Brian Bailey/Getty Images, p. 3; Allen Birnbach/Masterfile, pp. 4-5; Johner/Getty Images, pp. 6-7, 21; Paul Vozdic/Getty Images, pp. 8-9; Scott Markewitz/Getty Images, pp. 10-11, 12-13, 16-17; Sam Diephuis/Getty Images, p. 14; John Kelly/Getty Images, pp. 14-15; photo & co/Getty Images, pp. 18-19; Cannondale Bicycle Corporation, p. 20.